My Next 24

C.L. BLACK JR.

Fulton Books
Meadville, PA

Published by Fulton Books 2022

ISBN 979-8-88505-725-7 (paperback)
ISBN 979-8-88505-726-4 (digital)

Printed in the United States of America

CONTENTS

Preface..v

Introduction: What if I Die Today? vii

Chapter 1:   Did I Laugh This Day?................................1

Chapter 2:   What Did I Do for Myself Today?.....................5

Chapter 3:   What Did I Do for Others This Day?..................9

Chapter 4:   Feeling Accomplished...............................13

Chapter 5:   Mental Well-Being..................................17

Chapter 6:   Physical Well-Being................................21

Chapter 7:   Spiritual Well-Being...............................25

Chapter 8:   Time with Loved Ones...............................29

Chapter 9:   Keep Grinding in the 24 Cycle......................33

Chapter 10: Live My Dream This Day? 37

Chapter 11: Travel in the Mind (Bonus Chapter) 41

This book revolves around the premise of gaining more perspective on the twenty-four-hour period in which we live our current lives. My goal is to relate everyday experiences that will help establish a common ground for all to build upon. I truly believe the past is just the past, the future has not yet arrived, and the present is the only thing in our control. Actually, the present has a direct impact on how we perceive the past and the future. So why not *live* in your next twenty-four?

What if I Die Today?

This is the start of my second book to date. After *The Fundamental Rules 4 Kindergarten 101*, I felt compelled to carry this positive mental attitude over to what I call the twenty-four-hour cycle. It is going to be there right in your face, no matter what presuming we wake up. In which case, if we don't, it will not matter anyway because you will be dead! Not cool to really think about, I know, just a reality check and all the more reason to pay attention to the point I'm trying to make.

Jumping right in, let's say you did die, what would matter to you if you were to speak? If you were to give a eulogy for yourself, what would that sound like? I took an elective in college called death and dying, and one of the assignments was to do your own eulogy. Talk about creepy; however, it was very interesting and informative. It really made me think about everything from a different perspective. I was younger, so of course, what I thought about was a bit more superficial than now with some years of wisdom behind me.

To be fair, I think the parameters should entail my actual accomplishments and what could have been achieved. Kind of like the distance between potential and kinetic energy. This is an interesting concept when discussing the duration of your life. Obviously, we would want to mention a lot of things, but they must be summarized due to time constraints. That is why I believe just as you should make the fewest words go the furthest, the next twenty-four hours and how we perceive them is paramount!

C

Did I Laugh This Day?

Laughing is something that when it happens makes us feel good. So why would we not want to do more of that? It's not like we are taking drugs to feel this effect. These are naturally produced endorphins free and at our disposal. Life can most certainly get the best of us some days, and a laugh here and there can reciprocate. Yeah, how about we do a little bit of the ole lex talionis and fight fire with fire!

It all starts with *attitude* and how we perceive any given situation. There are many opportunities to take advantage of this great ability that has been given to us. We just have to recognize and create these moments and realize how important it is to our complete day.

It truly is amazing how something so basic can have such an impact on the way we carry out our mission in this world. It is a serious place we live in, and life itself is probably the most difficult combat sport of all. Let us be prepared to deal with it on our own terms as much as possible and kick it right in the ass!

It was a morning that I awoke early thinking of *everything*! And when I say everything, I mean literally all things out of my control. Usually, all kinds of thoughts of the past and the future, ranging from what I could have done better to what I may never encounter. I know it sounds crazy, right? But I'm not crazy because I know that you can relate, and that would make you crazy, and we can't have that now, can we? Maybe we are all crazy! Anyway, I'm lying there with this feeling of *my world* coming down on me, and I somehow have to snap out of it. By just getting out of bed is a start and allowing myself to begin my morning routine. As I allow this to happen, I find myself gaining some ground on the tension I have been exposed to with my thoughts. It is more of a negative feeling that can take me into a downward spiral and have an impact on the entire day.

Meanwhile, what is about to happen takes me on a different journey. I'm on my way to work, and I see this guy on a mountain bike riding alongside the road. And not just any road, it was a very busy stretch with a speed limit of forty-five miles per hour, which means fifty-five miles per hour to most people driving these days. I'm thinking to myself as I pass, *Why would someone put their life in jeopardy like this?*

As I pass, I notice he is an older man, and there is a storage rack on the back of his bike. This prompted me to go further into my procession of what I like to call merely an *observation*, not a judgment. So I'm trying to come up with reasons why this guy would be doing something so ridiculous.

And on the back of his bike, there was a rack that harnessed a thirty pack of natural ice beer and two cartons of his type of oxygen. Immediately, I thought, *Yeah, this guy recently acquired a DUI, and this is his primary source of transportation now.* The time is around 8:15 a.m., and the morning rush is in full effect.

Yes, this is a person willing to risk their life for chemical satisfaction at a cellular level and has this big ass smile on their face as I pass. And what was running through my mind at this point is, *What the hell am I watching right now?* As I look in my rearview mirror, I'm not really sure if I should feel sorry for this person or be jealous of their laissez-faire brush on the canvas of life.

But one thing is for certain here, I got an internal laugh that would blot out my morning of negative vibes. And this most definitely would have an impact on how I put things in perspective for the rest of my day. Two important things happened here that I will mention.

The first being that after I chuckled, I felt happy inside that I wasn't this person regardless of his lack of irresponsibility and neglect.

It was quite apparent to me that even though he appeared happy, there were many issues that needed to be addressed.

The second was a complete validation of how my attitude changed when I realized that I was in the present state of mind and not conducting thoughts from the past or future. This was comforting and allowed me to think about just how good my life really is right *now*! This train of thought may seem very primitive to you, but this is everything.

It is right in front of your face most of the time, and we fail to recognize it. Much like an opportunity standing, silently waiting for you to recognize it. Most think that it knocks on everybody's door. This is just not the case. We are actually taking a situation and using it to our benefit, kind of tricking yourself into a different type of mindset.

This is a way to impose the death penalty on these ghosts of thoughts that only we have the power to bring to life. I know that sounds a little deeper, but just as every action has an equal and opposite such is the case with our feelings. I don't know about you, but I'm seeking a high level of quality of life in my day that all starts with your own happiness. We must adopt more ways to improve on attaining this type of behavior. After all, if we do not have happiness or the ability to become happy, then what else is there?

What Did I Do for Myself Today?

This is a very interesting question when we clarify the difference between monetary, which can be a bit more superficial than something that is considered just plain old fun. Monetary meaning using money as a means of gaining some type of intrinsic need or want that will lead to satisfaction.

And having plain old fun or relaxation is more basic in form. Doing things for ourselves is great and should not be frowned upon. Obviously, this does not mean going out and spending a bunch of money on stuff that you can't afford but more along the lines of treating yourself to a gift of some sort.

This could be in the form of something that is as rewarding as a favorite snack or as basic as five real minutes of time in a relaxed state of mind. Both are considered ways of showing yourself gratitude and accomplish the goal of recognition without going overboard. As in anything consistency is crucial and essential to establish a pattern of goodness, we have earned the right to take advantage.

My twenty-four-hour cycle is interesting in the sense of what it entails. Kind of like certain factions broken down into groups ranging from responsibility to making time for myself. These are ever-changing because that is what life forces us to do. However, we can make adjustments to accommodate and maintain the cycle.

I consider anything that I normally would not do as actual work. The reason I feel this way is my perception of time and how valuable it is to me. We only have so much of it, and if we do not choose wisely, we could have consequences and/or ramifications that do not bode well for our growth.

Let us cite an example of doing something for yourself that you can relate to and imagine the possibilities. No matter what kind of somatotype you have the propensity to become in life—ectomorph (thin), endomorph (thicker), or mesomorph (muscular)—this simple example will apply, and I will show you how.

We all need to take care of our bodies mentally as well as physically. Jane Doe got up this morning and worked out a little harder than she normally would. Therefore, she lost a few more calories and really felt great to start the day. In the back of her mind, lingering was the thought of, *Maybe I can have a little treat later this evening.*

Is there a problem with this type of thinking? The answer is *no*! People in today's society just go plain apeshit on insane behavior that does not allow for healthy growth. Life is a test and a long one at that. We must make strides in increments that do not allow for failure to rear its ugly self!

Have you ever seen someone that has lost a whole bunch of weight in a short amount of time? Of course, you have, and you also have some thoughts of the before-and-after photos. Most of the time, what people think they should look like and what they do look like are two entirely different things, much like plastic surgery.

We tend to take it a bit too far at times, and most likely due to the fact that maybe this is something that has become very personal. And this is fine as long as we remember to make sure we receive the happiness we seek. It should not be ruined by a routine that becomes so arduous that it cancels out the very benefit we desire. Knowing our limitations can be a great deterrent in preserving our right to do something for ourselves and feel good about the reward.

This is the type of balance that we need so that internal growth can be achieved in a healthy manner. Remember, we are trying to establish a routine that will be attainable and sustainable. It is crucial to keep this a consistent piece of the fabric we are weaving in our quilt that comprises the twenty-four-hour cycle of success.

N

CHAPTER 3

What Did I Do for Others This Day?

By this, I mean literally anything that you would consider a random act of kindness. No deed is considered too small when doing something for someone that requires your time and effort because, remember, even though you are the giver, you are also the beneficiary of something special.

The feeling of completeness that we receive by doing for others is a gift that can be unparalleled. The problem is that most of us let our own selfishness supersede and rule our natural behavior. Not to be confused with chapter 2 when I required you to do something for yourself. If we are balanced in our twenty-four-hour cycle, then we are accomplishing both!

It is easy to become complacent and not do this on a consistent basis. Therefore, we must really be cognizant of the value in this need that can accomplish so much for us and our genetic fiber that was meant to be revealed by our creator.

It was a day much like others when I seemed rushed in my morning routine. I jump into the car, and *bam*, the gas light comes on! Now I'm kicking myself in the ass for not filling up the night before. I do not understand how this is physically possible, but I was doing it.

Anyway, I get to the gas station, and obviously, this puts me further behind in my timing. In the back of my mind, of course, I'm thinking and allowing myself to get caught up in being behind schedule. We all know this too well! It is very easy to displace aggression at this point, and all we need is a viable candidate.

No sooner said and an opportunity conveniently presents itself. A person needs someone to let them exit an area onto the main road, and of course, no one is obliging. It is my turn, and as I sigh, I yield and waive the person to exit. I could tell they were distressed, and who knows, maybe in more of a hurry than me.

As I was driving and thinking about what had just happened, I realized something. My feelings were confusing, to say the least. I lost track of the whole "being behind schedule" thing, and my mind truly wandered. I felt good about making a concession for someone, and this afforded me the luxury of a bit of euphoria.

This kind of balanced me much like a reset button had been pushed that I did not know existed. As I approached my destination and parked my car ready to enter the workplace, all vitals seemed to be normal.

Granted this was not the perfect morning, and I will probably be searching for that until the day I'm taken, but it was not a bad one either. I used a hidden technique, and it turned into somewhat of a superpower! I know it sounds crazy to think this way, but is it not just as crazy to get yourself all worked up and drive like a maniac to what? Make yourself feel better? Put others in danger?

The reason this sounds so stupid to rationalize is that most of us are too stupid to realize the fundamentals. This is as basic as it gets yet so difficult to actually manifest. Isn't that the way life is designed most of the time? Simple yet effective strategies that get the job done!

This situation allowed me to adapt my behavior and utilize my hidden resource center to act as a counter deterrent. Basically, I was able to grow in my own way without any bias from others, and just knowing that I have the power to do this is so rewarding.

Most of the time, we get so caught up in the moment that we tend to follow the normal protocol. And doesn't that just get old? Challenge yourself to get better and demand the best possible outcome. Do not lower yourself to other people's level of behavior or expectations.

I know this sounds kind of brutal in nature, but that is just the way it is. You have to be tough on yourself because life is the true contact sport! Obviously, my example cited was a spontaneous act, and I'm making a big deal about it because I want to share my realization of an opportunity for all to take advantage.

S

Feeling Accomplished

Wow! How many days go by before we ask ourselves this question. How did I do this day? Or actually evaluate our individual performance from the inside. If you're reading this book, it is clearly an indication that you want to better yourself. And I want to bring this train of thought to the surface and be your *best friend of help*!

A performance evaluation of yourself requires a great deal of honesty and willingness to grow. Not many of us get to this point due to the fact that we tend to not want to reveal the truth about our day, as if there is a practice in session and we are kind of going through the motions if you will to just get through it.

Unfortunately, this type of thinking is counterproductive because we do not bring out the best in us. To carry this analogy between practice and daily evaluation further. What do you think happens when people train in a sport and the effort put forth is minimal? Like doing half the reps required in any given activity?

I will tell you what happens. You become lazy and complacent, and any competition you are training for is at risk of failure. Why would we not treat our day as such and make the adjustments to improve so that we are able to kick it right in the *ass*?

Have you ever gone to sleep at night and felt like your day was incomplete? There are times when I feel this way, and it usually revolves around not getting things done that I did not want to do. People, in general, have a tendency to put aside or avoid situations that are threatening our homeostasis. That is our normal state of being

I will share an example of mine to relate this mentality to our twenty-four-hour cycle. I have worked in sales for quite some time, and I'm very old school when it comes to my prospecting of potential customers. To be honest, I wasn't sold (Ha!) on the idea as a profession when I got started.

Over time, I realized that this was an art just like any other job. And salespeople are needed just as much as custodians. When I use the word art, I mean it as a way we perceive this in our minds. We can literally make anything an art and follow a certain protocol for success.

My job requires many different types of prospecting—one of which is telemarketing. Please don't hold this against me! All I was trying to do is hold a conversation and establish some type of common ground to earn trust. No, that is not a crock of shit I just fed you. Now that wouldn't be nice, would it?

Anyway, when I first started this type of lead generation, it was a bit intimidating because of the amount of rejection that was involved. I soon began dreading it and was just going through the motions, and I realized something. Hey, dumbass, if your paycheck is your motivation and you are on all commission, then you need to change your mindset.

And that is exactly what I did! I started making it a challenge and holding myself accountable. When someone hung up on me or used profanity, I began to use it as fuel for my next call. I made a conscious choice to exit the conversation with an inner smile on my face. This allowed me to not take it personally and stay positive.

Soon, everything became what I like to call a *persistent consistency*! If we can apply this combination to the things we dislike most, then the protocol will take care of the rest. Now don't get me wrong here. I had days prior and post that did not employ this tactful practice. Obviously, these were the days where I felt less accomplished and more like I bitched out!

The reason I'm using this example is that we need to work on the things that we fear the most. It is generally what everyone else tries to avoid and ultimately what leads to success. This is a fact, and by doing will contribute greatly to the feeling of being accomplished in your twenty-four-hour cycle.

There will be times when fear and doubt creep in and have a direct impact on our daily performance. But let us realize that these are things in our control! These are things that do not exist unless we allow them to exist. We actually give them power over us, and before we know it, there we are in a submissive state of mind. Kind of makes you think about it when brought forth in this manner, right?

The bottom line here is that there is already enough leverage in this world out of our control that does not leave too much room for error if we wish for success. So be sure to keep the odds in your favor by staying positive and focused and the art of feeling accomplished will be at your mercy.

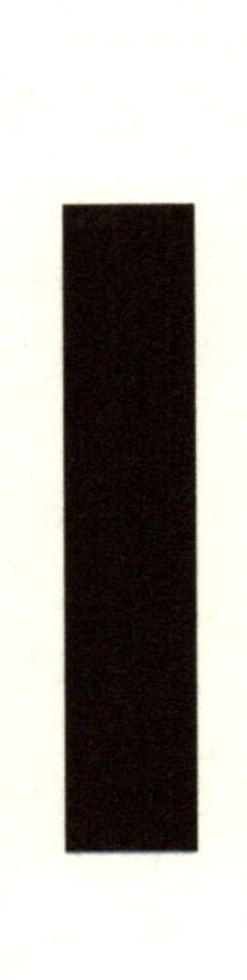

Mental Well-Being

And when I say mental well-being, what do I mean? Our ability to feel balanced in any given situation we may encounter in our twenty-four-hour cycle. This is something so vital to our health it is not even close when comparing to other priorities.

I remember in health class many years ago, the teacher saying that the silent killer of stress was the number 1 killer on the planet. I thought to myself, *There is no way this is accurate, considering all the other things that people do on a daily basis to kill themselves.* Now that I'm older and realize just what real stress is, *I know this to be true!*

Have you ever heard the expression "Kill the head kill the body"? This is what we are discussing here, and it plays a very significant role in our everyday life. We, as humans, tend to look at things from the outside when, in fact, the inside is the control room.

Why do we do this? My guess would be that society and all its great pressures to be something that is acceptable to everyone else. That is purely sad, is it not? Especially when all of us are created uniquely and have the ability to bring to life something special.

We have to take care of ourselves mentally, or everything else will eventually suffer, and failure is imminent. A good example that applies here is the expression "Looks like somebody woke up on the wrong side of the bed." Now what the hell is that supposed to mean? If we actually allow this to sink in and think it's going to be a shitty day, I can almost guarantee you it is going to be a shitty day!

Obviously, I have an example in mind to paint this lovely portrait for all to admire. An anonymous person is having the above-mentioned day and really needs some sort of glimmer of hope. Where can they find it? Most of the time, we allow ourselves to slip into this domino effect of everything left to conquer in our day.

This person has had one hell of a day, and it all started by hitting the sleep button instead of the snooze. They got behind schedule and never really caught up, and this brought on feelings of stress. It is amazing how something so basic can lead to what seems like a catastrophic event.

In their mind, everything was a rush because they were behind from the start. This is, of course, unconscious preemptive thought behavior that is the culprit and can really be persuasive. At this juncture, it is imperative that we have a "go-to plan" of action, which is primarily one of the reasons I decided to write this book.

The go-to plan starts with us realizing that we have to hit a reset button internally to break the negative cycle we are experiencing. This could be something as simple as a few deep breaths through the nose and out the mouth and focusing on something positive. Or maybe we reflect on something positive that has happened in our lives and we are very thankful. Another thought is considering how fortunate we are compared to others who may be in adverse conditions.

Are you picking up what I'm putting down here? These are all effective means of snapping back into the mental state of mind that is required to be on top of your game, so to speak. Still, even if none of this is applied and your go-to plan just plain sucks, a victory can be achieved.

Try to focus on the fact that you are still in a very successful twenty-four-hour cycle that promotes a guarantee of minimal damage. In other words, there are a lot of other things that you will accomplish throughout your day, and this will ensure a positive outlook.

By staying in your productive routine in this twenty-four-hour cycle, you can rebound quickly and use momentum as something to build upon. We cannot afford to allow ourselves to fall victim to even the smallest of change.

We must adapt and move in the right direction mentally. This is huge in pretty much everything we will encounter in this contact sport of life. Would you agree that it is better to be an agent of change rather than presumed dead as a victim of change?

S

Physical Well-Being

When considering our ability to be as productive as possible, we must put into place some type of fitness parameters that require consistency. Also, this must be a plan of action that is attainable and not too overwhelming. This is important so that we can adopt normalcy, such as an engine that starts when commanded on a daily basis.

Taking care of yourself physically is one of the best things you can do for yourself and others you love. It is something that is within our control to take advantage of and benefit from in many ways. I can't speak for you, but I'm all about the quality of life, and general fitness can promote and sustain this if used in the right way.

The main benefit of exercise is obvious, such as appearance that revolves around toning, weight loss, strength, etc., and usually the main reason people get started on a regimen. Also, conversely, the reason people do not succeed, and it is short-lived. Why? Primarily due to the fact that this is more superficial in nature.

This is not to say that these benefits do not matter; however, I'm more interested in the endorphin release and the impact it can have on us mentally that sets the tone for the day. Make sense? The mindset here is that we are doing something for ourselves that nobody can take from us. No matter what adverse conditions we encounter this day, we are making sure that at least one thing in our control is a success.

This is very important to realize and something most who even take advantage of—do not use as a cornerstone for mental growth. Why? Because, again, we tend to think of fitness as a more physical than mental need, and this is just not the case. In fact, I would say for me if I were to measure in percentage, probably 75 percent mental.

I believe this is the case for this simple reason. We are obviously getting a physical benefit from exercise by just doing it. However, if we are staying in our routine and getting the mental clarity that we need, then we are going to feel better about ourselves in general and so forth.

This leads me to my next point. Too much of anything is bad! People who tend to go overboard with the fitness regimen are in danger of being out of balance mentally. When your whole day is revolving around, one thing it is not good.

For example, Jane Doe runs—I mean runs a hell of a lot! But she runs so much that it is more of a deterrent throughout her day because of the pressure of getting in X amount of miles.

This is not to say that Jane should not look forward to her run and want to do well. It is merely pointing out that one thing should not dominate the majority of your twenty-four-hour cycle. Balance is so crucial, and many have said this in the past, but it is more difficult than we think primarily due to our inability to determine what I just mentioned.

It is very easy to get focused on one area and think we are being successful. True success is accomplished from within and not by others or their feelings and thoughts toward you. It is an incremental process that is almost unidentifiable because it happens consistently over a period—much like the tortoise when compared to the hare in a race.

A lot of people always discuss how others have beat the odds when talking about living their lives a certain way. For example, people who do not take care of themselves by being sedentary and having horrible habits. Someone who, let's say, smokes and drinks excessively to the point of embarrassment lives to be like ninety years old.

Well, this may happen but more than likely not often. I would venture to say that this person's quality of life may have suffered in many ways even though they lived a long life. But then again, I truly feel longevity is really how you live your life and not just a number. Think about it!

In either event, when I wake up in the morning, I'm not banking on the fact that I will have a traumatic ending this day. So I'm going to do whatever I can within my control to take advantage of bettering myself. And if this was my last day, then I was on the right path of purpose and not subjecting myself to other self-inflicting wounds to determine my fate.

This is a pure serenity prayer mentality. Something I will write specifically about in the near future. It is very simple. Grant me the serenity to accept the things I cannot change, the courage to change the things I can, and the wisdom to know the difference. Basically, in my twenty-four-hour cycle, I want to control what I can to make a difference in my quality of life.

T

Spiritual Well-Being

Now this is an area that most of us tend to push aside and not prioritize at times. What I mean by this is that our intentions may be good, but following through is another level of commitment—a whole new level that needs to be explored and is relative to self-accountability.

This means taking initiative and making it happen on a regular basis. I find myself thinking of the way it was before I began my journey of improvement. Even though I felt some type of void, I was clueless of how to fill it. I know that many of us can relate to this, and it is very easy to escape from our busy schedules.

The reason for this is that in general people do not understand this concept. We confuse spiritual well-being with church and characterize it as a duty. If used correctly, it becomes a need and something that is a priority in our twenty-four-hour cycle.

First, we must understand exactly what comprises this realm of thought and be cognizant of the benefits we receive. When thinking of spiritual well-being, I'm not talking about going to church every Sunday and trying to remember the message that was conveyed.

What I'm more interested in is making the time to do this on your own and on a regular basis. Autonomy in this manner is extremely fulfilling and can promote a higher level of knowledge and understanding. Why? Because of your *own* initiative, and this will most certainly lead to self-accountability. Such a very awful thing these days, isn't it?

I know everyone is born with the intrinsic need to do well. But this is only possible if we are willing to do the things necessary today that most will not do to acquire the things tomorrow most will not have. In other words, life just doesn't work out perfectly. *You* have to invest your time and effort in a consistent and persistent manner.

Trust me here, I know what I'm talking about based on tenure in this realm. Throughout my life, I have tested the waters, so to speak, and why would I write about false information that would lead others astray? I wouldn't! So please pay attention and learn from my trials.

I would suggest trying to establish some type of prayer that is uniform in nature. And something that *you* took the time to establish in your own words that are true and meaningful. The beauty in this is that it will give you strength and confidence that was hidden deep down in your awesome soul.

People who doubt prayer are narrow-minded and in hiding from their true self. That is just the way it is! Why? Because it is a viable threat to their everyday fraudulent happiness. I know this sounds abrasive, but life with accountability has a way of escaping us without consequence.

Along with prayer as a guide, try to make some time to actually study the Word of God. Our God wants us to show that we are willing to understand the instructional manual of life known as the Bible. Once you take initiative on a consistent basis, things will happen in a guiding fashion. This is just like anything else in life. If you expect to excel at something, you must make the time and effort.

And yes, I know there are a lot of people who cannot stick to reading this material, such as *me*. But trying to read and retain this material led me to the audio version, which was a saving grace. I know it sounds ridiculous, but even though I write, my way of learning is primarily audio/video.

I'm literally telling you what I know from experience and work on myself. As they say, "Gloves are off," and I want you to understand that I'm here as an active tutor who wants the best for you. Think of it this way. My tenure of idiocy and random misfortune will be your guide. And hopefully, you will not have to endure too much before you get to the place in life you need to be. However, if this is not the case, learn and grow and *adapt*!

E

Time with Loved Ones

In this world of chaos surrounded by others who dictate a pace so fast, sometimes it seems near impossible to keep up. Our minds get caught up in a cycle that promotes a heightened state of paranoia. This can lead to an array of dysfunctional efforts in our twenty-four-hour cycle.

The time, we make for the people in our lives that make a difference can be almost invisible to us, given the world and its "life goes on" theme! Have you ever wondered why you have not heard or spoken to someone you are very close to in quite some time? Does this become a dual between the two of you that revolves around who will touch base first? Maybe you're not on good terms or have just drifted apart.

Whatever the case, it is a good idea to try to make an effort to stay in touch on a regular basis, and the frequency depends on what faction they reside in your world. For example, people you are around daily, people you are around rarely, or people who just may need you. All these individuals deserve some type of attention, and even though our intentions are good, we must follow through.

Why? Because this can play a role in the ability to function at a higher level in our twenty-four-hour cycle. Consider it another variable that can be interchangeable and leaves no void yet makes us feel complete at times. We are very intricate and unique in ways many of us do not completely comprehend.

Little things like taking the time to share thoughts and experiences with the people we love the most are essential. It all adds up over time and has a positive impact on our ability to function. Also, the gift of sharing time with others is immense. It is important to remember this reciprocity and hold yourself to some type of accountability on a regular basis.

All our situations are most likely different when exploring this basic expectation. A lot of factors can play a role in the ability to make this time, such as job demands that may require longer hours and or commutes. We must be cognizant of these time constraints and take advantage of the possibility to *make time*!

If not, this will certainly multiply and eventually become the cause of many issues that could have been prevented by examining our *next* twenty-four! All we have to do is make the adjustments necessary and a great night of sleep will await us. I love the fact that when my head hits the pillow, I have no regrets. And isn't that what it's all about? Going back to what if I die today?

Well, if this is the case, then at least feel complete in your efforts that are in your control. Obviously, there are times when factors out of our control take hold and are directly the cause of interference. Do not fret, my friends, this is no reason to feel like we are inadequate. Do not let this overcome your emotional state and become burdensome.

This would be the opposite of what we are trying to accomplish here on a regular basis, right? I will give an example of a situation that might make this clearer for you. This will relate to the faction of someone close to you that you may see on a more frequent or daily basis.

It is the weekend, and you have made it through a solid week of hell. A week that really tested your code of ethics when dealing with life in general. There are several different things you would like to do to decompress and somewhat purge from this mental anguish. Things that just may not include anyone including the closest people in your life.

Typically, during the week, you get home with little time to spend with your family in the evenings. But you do spend time, and even though it might be limited, it is quality time. Lately, this time has been devoted to playing a board game that did not seem to get finished Friday evening.

Make this a priority over the weekend to finish the game and maybe even start another. You will be surprised at the impact it can have on your attitude toward everything. Even though it was not your intention from the start, it will bleed over and make the necessary difference.

This is not to say that we still don't seek out our decompression chamber. What I'm pointing out here is that having this type of mindset is therapeutic in ways that you may not realize. Remember, it's the big picture we are faced with on a daily basis that obviously can be overwhelming *all* the time, if and only if we allow for it!

This can also play a major role when considering the other factions of people you might want to create time for. This freedom of making time for your loved ones can give merit to the other factions at their discretion. In other words, this can build confidence to reach out and make the time that was seemingly unavailable.

Whether it be someone you were close to in the past or someone that may need your advice and or attention, you can at least have the option to act on and not have any reservations that will ultimately affect your emotional state.

This is what I am after—the type of thinking that can and will set the tone for the upcoming week. And as each week passes, we can get more and more aquatinted with our regimen for success. The type of success that comes from within, which is the most gratifying of all.

Keep Grinding in the 24 Cycle

I know this sounds like a *raw* term to most, but that is how it should sound. Grinding is something that we tend to shy away from because it requires a great deal of primitive commitment. What I mean by that is that it is associated with the very things in life that we dislike.

People who grind on a daily basis probably cannot relate to this because they have already been through the gauntlet of transformation. In other words, they are so entrenched in their twenty-four-hour cycle that it becomes second nature. And if they are reading this book, it would be for pure validation of their efforts.

Okay, so what does grinding entail? Well, I would say the ability to do the following. As the famously renowned logo says, "Just Do It!" I would add to that by saying, "Just Get Off Your Ass and Do It!" It might sound a bit harsh and probably won't be PC these days, but then again, I don't give a——!

I'm not here to paint this beautiful portrait of accountability. I'm here to instill an awakening of sorts. Sometimes being abrasive in situational life can be the game-changing element needed to take the next step to ascendancy.

The problem we encounter most of the time is that people generally do not like to travel outside of their comfort zone. Obviously, this is the primary cause of the inability to excel. Why? Because we are content with the finite limits that we are confined to by this type of thinking.

We have to break the cycle, and as Andy Dufresne said in *The Shawshank Redemption*, "Get busy living or get busy dying!" If you really think about it here, this applies perfectly to what I'm trying to explain. The grinding effect is almost unnoticeable at times because this is a slow grind.

A grind that we keep doing over a period due to our consistent efforts amounts to something. Does this make sense? In other words, if we keep our nose to the grindstone in our twenty-four-hour cycle, at some point, this is going to amount to a positive result.

We just can't afford to think about all the deterrent boundaries that we tend to allow for ourselves. Complacency is the real enemy here, and we have the power to overcome these mental barriers. It truly is one of life's little secrets that many will never encounter due to an inconsistent pattern of behavior.

The success as a whole that will ultimately prevail from your efforts is not to be confused with increments of losses or gains. Basically, try not to think about the fact that *all* things in our twenty-four-hour cycle have to be improving constantly. This can lead to burnout and be somewhat demoralizing.

We do not want to go "against the grind" here! Ha! Think of it kind of like someone who wants to go on a diet and lose a few pounds. If they choose to go crazy and limit their calories too much, what do you think is going to happen? Most likely, a relapse is right around the corner to rear its ugly self.

Everything in moderation is actually a great example of this type of mental process, and it is at its core. There are times when we are not going to feel like doing more this day, and this is okay. Kind of like a cheat day on this hypothetical diet. On the contrary, we might experience days of thunder where we want to do extra. The key here is *balance* at its most primitive level.

I will leave you with this to ponder when considering your grind mentality. Everything since the day we were born is a learned process. Would you agree that we were all born dumb, naked, and speechless? Then yes, we are on the same page. Since we have entered this world, everything adds to our primitive and necessary level of function.

I'm personally here to tell you that the more we ignore the fundamental basic structure, the more we hinder the total function. The structure represents our anatomy, and the function is our physiology. My point being that it would be impossible to function efficiently without structure. Imagine the organs in your body functioning without the bone structure to support them. Get it?

C

Live My Dream This Day?

No matter who you are in this world, dreams of becoming something people consider special are indeed imminent. There is no timetable as to how we should pursue these dreams—just an internal calling that they exist. The key is to make a decision to set the plan in motion.

Sounds so easy and like I have it all figured out, right? This is definitely not the case; otherwise, more than 2 percent of the population would live their dreams. But then again, I stand corrected when I say it is that easy to make a decision and act on our dreams. The problem is the fear of failure we create and will have to endure while trying to reach them.

This fear can be and act like a silent killer in ways that are unnoticeable because we tend to view our goals as one big dream. In reality, they are comprised of a series of smaller ones that reach this goal. I like to equate it to a war that has many little battles leading up to *victory*.

So then how does one live their dream this day if we are not there yet? And the answer is simple, *incrementally*. We have to be *patiently aggressive*! This is where most people fail when striving to reach their dreams. They view this dream as one big entity, and it becomes such an overwhelming obstacle.

By employing this technique of being *patiently aggressive*, I truly feel the probability of success becomes greater.

The patience part is a mental restrain from doing too much in this area that it becomes a factor and has an effect on other areas and upsetting the twenty-four-hour cycle of balance. The aggressive part is keeping this in mind but challenging yourself to stay with it on a regular basis. As maybe an older wise person would suggest, *operation widdle it away!*

By doing this on a regular basis, we are actually living a part of our dream every day. Are you picking up what I'm putting down here? What most of us fail to understand is how important the journey to our dreams is to the dream itself. There is a reason why people say "enjoy the journey."

This journey is what we will cling to when it is all said and done. Once the pinnacle has been reached, it's amazing how successful people reminisce over the journey. And the great thing about your mindset of achievement here is that it is not about the end. In fact, quite the contrary.

If you are constantly trying to achieve this dream, your mindset will be healthy, and in reality, you are living your dream by doing what is necessary to improve. Let us keep in mind that opportunity does not knock on everybody's door. *Oh no!* Opportunity stands alone in a dormant realm, waiting for you to recognize it!

This is a very different mindset indeed to comprehend due to the fact that society has it all wrong. We really have to challenge ourselves to a higher level of thinking and, most importantly, *act* on it! To live your dream is no joke! We have to answer that internal calling and travel to that place in our minds.

Did you ever wonder what people actually mean when they say, "You can do anything if you just put your mind to it"? And most of us that hear that saying never really take it seriously, and do you know why? Because it's a bullshit saying. That is why!

The reason I believe this, is that because most people who say this, are generalizing and not being more specific. It is used as a motivational weapon to get us to seek out the battle. The problem is that this is an easy argument to dispute and rationalize as a false statement. Maybe a better saying would be, "You can do anything if you just *believe in your mind!*"

For example, someone who has a severe disability and is in a wheelchair could hear this and say, "I want to walk again." Well, the only way this is possible would be if they travel in their mind to a place they see themselves walking. Does that make sense? We have to really differentiate here when referring to the word *mind*.

This will allow people to grasp this basic concept that most of the time is *void* of the basics. Once this is recognized, then we can begin to build on and use it as an everyday mental tool for our work to be done. Give ourselves that extra kick in the ass that no one else can do!

The *realization* of living your dream on a daily basis is a part of the twenty-four-hour cycle that is rarely traveled. Once the pinnacle has been reached, we tend to look at the beginning and then the finished product. I think it is imperative to *brand* the journey deep in our minds so that complacency never becomes an issue. Hence, we never forget where we came from! And always remember, my friends, living your dream has nothing to do with monetary value and everything to do with your *happiness*!

Y

Travel in the Mind (Bonus Chapter)

As I mentioned earlier, to travel in the mind is a rarity. And no, I do not mean experimenting with some type of hallucinogenic drug. This idea revolves around us, making time to seek out our God-given creativity. We all have *special gifts* that may or may not be attached to an internal calling.

Whatever the case, we need to eventually harness this type of mentality for it is in jeopardy of being lost forever when we pass. And what if this is something that may help others for years to come and we choose to keep it hidden from us because of our own negligence.

I don't think I want that haunting my conscience on a daily basis. This feeling of I should've, could've, would've, but *I did not*! So how do we get out of this mindset of thinking that is crippling and interfering with our travels to higher ground?

I feel that if we can go to this place of I can, I will, I must, on a consistent basis, then some type of blueprint will manifest. Make no mistake about it, success begins with a *solid will*. It is all in a state of mind! But first, we must have the ability to *believe* in ourselves. Confidence will breed confidence, and the rest will be just a reminder of making your life *yours*!

Now where the hell is this place I keep referring to and you are confused about? Obviously, a realm somewhere deep in your mind that you and only *you* can travel to. This is a *haven of potential* that can only be transformed into *kinetic* by your efforts. The key is to *believe* in yourself and make a conscious consistent effort.

I remember when I had days that tested my spirit so much that it actually turned into a cycle of chaos. The outside world pushing and pulling me like some kind of freakish bully. To fight back meant that I had to develop some kind of strategy to protect and prevent a complete rupture.

Being preemptive can only get you so far. You have to actually experience the hardships to endure and grow. This is what everyone talks about when they say "Walk a mile in my shoes." When I think about this particular dilemma, one glaring work of art comes to mind: *the serenity prayer*!

In this cycle of chaos I was confounded to, I used this as a vehicle to the sanctuary. I know this sounds a bit "out there," but I'm just trying to be as transparent as possible. Maybe inside, you are already feeling great about yourself due to how——up I was at one time.

I would literally go to my basement and lie down and recite this prayer over and over while breathing through my nose and out my mouth. It was a form of meditation that became therapeutic in nature and made a difference.

What I'm getting at here is that you need to find a decompression chamber of sorts for yourself. This can serve as a type of voluntary defense mechanism to prepare for daily warfare. As they say, "The best offense is a good defense," and this certainly applies to the *real* combat sport called *life*!

With stress being the number 1 killer, I would think that happiness would be the number 1 antidote. Why not employ some type of strategy to go to a place where you can feel whole again? Get grounded and know that you are being proactive in changing your life parameters. Not life itself dictating all that happens and making it up as it happens.

I always hear people say, "It is what it is," and that drives me insane. What the hell does that mean? That is totally taking the mindset of failure! The saying should be, "It is what you make it!" Now that is the mindset of someone who is going to find a way to *make* things happen!

Are not the tides of life and all it has to offer jaded a bit? Can we really afford to think in this manner and expect success to knock on our door? Absolutely *not*! Self-accountability is the only way to recognize the path of righteousness. Probably the best words that ever made sense in a rap song were "Success is my only option, failure's not! What a great lyric in the song "Lose Yourself!"

My friends, I will leave you with this analogy.

Consider life as a continuous game of tag and your twenty-four hour cycle as *home base*!

ABOUT THE AUTHOR

C.L. Black Jr. is a tenured and successful business owner who resides in Virginia. He grew up in Baltimore City and graduated from The Milton Hershey School an orphanage in Pennsylvania. Overcoming adversity and defying the norm have become a habitual sanctuary for Charles. In fact, He would like to submit a formal change for the well known term Murphey's Law to Murphey's Lineage!